An Architectural Journey Through Long Island

AUGUST VIEMEISTER

An Architectural Journey Through Long Island

Edited with an Introduction by **MARIAN LEIFSEN**

PUBLISHED BY KENNIKAT PRESS / PORT WASHINGTON, NEW YORK
UNDER THE AEGIS OF THE LONG ISLAND CHAPTER
OF THE AMERICAN INSTITUTE OF ARCHITECTS

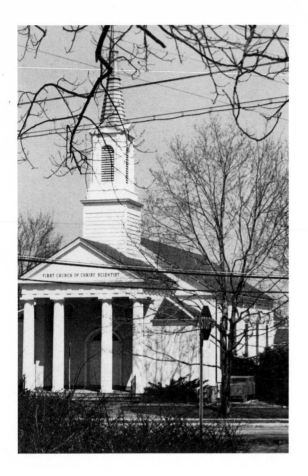

ISBN: 0−8046−9109−6

Manufactured in the United States of America

Published by
Kennikat Press Corp.
Port Washington, N. Y. / London

TO MY DARLING

J.E.V

Contents:

Early American Homes   1

Early American Inns   37

Places of Worship   41

Lighthouses and Towers   59

Residences   65

Clubs and Recreation   75

Long Island from the Air   87

Old Bethpage   97

Educational Facilities   105

Land and Seascapes   119

Commerce and Industry   127

Index   148

Preface

One day, not too long ago, at a meeting of the Long Island
Chapter of the American Institute of Architects, members
of the historic preservation committee were talking about
making some kind of a record of the development of architecture on Long Island. Books had been published about
architecture in other areas, but nowhere was there a complete picture, an illustrated history of architecture here.

August Viemeister, a member in long standing, was not
one to sit around talking about it. He decided the project
needed doing and he would do it. So, at the age of 80 he
enrolled in an adult education class and learned how to use a
camera. Once satisfied that he could capture the island's
architectural style on film, and armed with a new camera and
a pile of notebooks, this peripatetic architect got into his car
and for the next three years traveled from one end of the
island to the other and back again until he had photographed
every house, church, inn, school, and commercial building
that he felt was representative of the history of architecture
on Long Island. He did quite a thorough job of it, for his
history includes the first houses ever built on the island, the
wide range of styles of today, and all that went between.

Typically modest, August Viemeister, now a member
emeritus, A.I.A., includes only one of his own designs in
An Architectural Journey Through Long Island—a bank in
Riverhead he designed while associated with architects
Holmes & Wright. But there are over one hundred buildings
on Long Island that are the result of August Viemeister's art
including twenty "country" homes in Roslyn Estates and his
own home and fire station in Dix Hills.

Born in 1893 in Brooklyn, August Viemeister came to
Roslyn as a child and has lived in Nassau or Suffolk ever
since. He was a member of the class of 1916 of the University of Pennsylvania and that same year designed a new home
for his mother in Roslyn. Members of his family still occupy
the house. In 1922 he earned his license to practice architecture professionally and has been doing it for fifty-two
years. As chief designer for Emery Roth & Sons, in New
York City, August Viemeister's credits include scores of
offices and apartment buildings and hotels. The Ritz Tower
is one of them.

So, with a vast store of experience as his guide, and love
of his art and Long Island as his inspiration, August Viemeister has captured the essence of the island's architecture.
Patiently cataloguing, labeling, and numbering each photo-
graph, and gathering information from town and village
historical societies whose enthusiastic help is acknowledged,
August Viemeister's *Architectural Journey Through Long
Island* is complete.

Some of the photographs were borrowed from a 1971
exhibit at Huntington's Heckscher Museum called "The
Architecture of Suffolk County." For these, deep apprecia-
tion is expressed to Eve Gatling, the museum's director.
Credits for some other professionally taken photographs
appear elsewhere.

So, turn the page and begin your journey through three
centuries of architecture—from the first "salt-box" built in
Cutchogue in 1649 to the more regal estates of wealthy land-
owners in pre-Revolutionary days who built Georgian colonial
mansions with slave labor and Indians. Its all here, the famous
octagonal houses, the Federal styles of the early nineteenth
century, the sturdy gambrel-roofed Dutch houses signified
by the front porch or "stoep" as they called it. The flam-
boyant Gold Coast era of the early twentieth century brought
with it some outrageously elaborate castle-like estates on the
north shore.

The influence of those durable early homes, fashioned by
farmers, fishermen and shipbuilders, who designed and built
homes for their own particular needs, is still obvious in
today's design. The colonial style house is the most popular
in suburban developments and there is little variation from
the original model. Compare the Thompson House in
Setauket, built around 1700, with the modern beach house
of artist Robert Gwathmey built in 1965. Though one is a
modest farmhouse built with available resources and the
other is ultra modern, the similarity in the simplicity of line
and form is there.

Before your journey is through you will probably find a
home in this book similar to your own. Take a look.

M. L.

Early American Homes

HOME SWEET HOME

Historians disagree as to whether John Howard Payne's birth in 1791 took place in this East Hampton saltbox cottage, or whether the Payne family left the area before his birth. All agree, however, that he did spend considerable time in East Hampton. Payne's interest in writing and acting started early, but his father, a teacher at nearby Clinton Academy, posed strong objections to such folly. Young Payne postponed his acting career and attended college. His yearning for the theatre got the best of him and after two years of college he gave up his formal education to make his way on the stage.

Probably the greatest event in Payne's career occurred in 1823 when *Clari* or *The Maid of Milan* opened at London's Covent Garden. The opera, written in collaboration with composer Henry Rowley Bishop, was well-received and the theme song "Home Sweet Home" was an instant hit.

It is this haunting song that links Payne most closely with East Hampton, a village which has become a summer mecca for artists, writers and actors. It was here that Payne, as a child, shared secrets, frolicked on the shore and explored the meadow with his cousin Clari until her death at the age of eight. The poet never forgot her, and "Home Sweet Home" in a very real sense, belongs to Clari and East Hampton.

The house, built in 1660, has been preserved as a museum with mementoes of Payne's career and family memorabilia on display.

GILBERT POTTER HOUSE

Despite protests from the Huntington historian, this noble Colonial mansion built by Gilbert Potter prior to 1786, was torn down in June 1974. The Greek Revival style house at 11 Wall Street had been used as a boarding house in recent years, and the owner sold it to an anxious buyer who wanted the site for commercial use. In fact, the house was sold so quickly that one of its boarders who had gone away for a few days returned to Huntington and found his home had disappeared, along with all his possessions.

CARLL HOMESTEAD

The Library of Congress has detailed plans on this house at 49 Melville Road in Huntington because it is the only house of its period with overhang from the second story. The Carll family built the house in 1680. It was recently purchased by Mr. and Mrs. E. Lowry who are restoring it to its original style.

WILLOW MERE

This majestic pre-Revolutionary mansion was built on a 250-acre shorefront setting in Roslyn. It was held by the Pearsall family until 1839 when Tom and Lavinia Pearsall were forced to give it up to creditors. The present owner, Jay Kauffman, who appreciates the folklore attached to Willow Mere, said that British soldiers approaching the house by boat were frightened away when servants rang the old bell on the roof which was used to call the farmhands to dinner. Kauffman also discovered that one of the dozen or so fireplaces enclosed a secret stairway for easy escape to the cellar and out to the harbor.

CARLL—MARION FARM

This early eighteenth century farmhouse on Commack Road, one mile south of Jericho Turn-pike, is now part of the Commack Hills Country Club. The brackets for the front columns as well as the roof eaves, reveal Italianate design.

VALENTINE HOUSE

A striking example of the Federal style is the William M. Valentine house on Paper Mill Road, Roslyn. Built in 1800 with additions in 1865, the house is now the Roslyn Village Hall.

COLYER HOUSE

Walt Whitman's father was a carpenter and this is one of the houses he built in Huntington. The house, very similar to the one he built for his own family, is set on a hill at 26 Mount Misery Road, and the interior as well as the exterior has been painstakingly preserved. The house was built in 1819 and is currently owned by a New York banker.

L'HOMMEDIEU HOUSE

This simple straightforward house with white painted siding was built in 1825 at 127 Old Country Road, Melville, by the L'Hommedieu family.

HEWLETT HOUSE

The first Hewletts settled in Hempstead in 1657 and the family later branched out to the north and south shores. This residence, at 559 Woodbury Road, Huntington, is now owned by Lloyd D. Bucher. Other Hewlett homesteads, built in 1725 and 1790, still stand in Port Washington. The house built in 1725 has been in continuous ownership of the Lewis Hewlett descendants, and is now owned by Lewis Hewlett and his sister Elizabeth Hewlett Hopkins.

BUFFET HOUSE

There were two Buffet houses built on West Rogues Path in Huntington. This one with hand hewn oak interior structure is number 159 and is currently owned by the Tortora family. It was built in the early 1800s.

SOLOMON SMITH HOUSE

On the south side of High Hold Drive in Huntington stands the Solomon Smith House, one of the few unspoiled original Colonial houses so typical of the 18th century with true lines, high chimneys, wrought iron hardware, and intricate interior moldings.

The house is said to have been sold only twice since its construction. Henry Stimson, who was secretary of war in the cabinets of several presidents, bought the estate from Smith. Stimson's estate was later sold to the Henry Kaufman Boy Scout Camp.

The fireplace on the left is an example of the preserved interiors of the house. The cambered brick opening, more than six-feet wide, has a movable wrought iron derrick bracket to adjust the cookpot to the fire. Vertical paneling of painted wooden boards complete the picture. The interior ceiling beams are hand adzed oak and some of the pine floor boards are over a foot wide.

Suffolk County is reportedly trying to acquire the estate for use as a public park.

OLD BUFFET HOUSE

This homestead built in 1776, at 169 West Rogues Path in Huntington, is the oldest Buffet home. The house boasts five chimneys, irregularly spaced second floor windows and a solid stone foundation. A soldier who died in the Revolutionary War is buried in the small graveyard behind the house.

CORNELIA PRIME HOUSE

Cornelia Prime was a Huntington benefactor who donated the memorial building and clock to the town. The house she lived in around the turn of the century, was built in 1848 by Moses Rolph, Huntington Town Clerk. Three generations of Rolphs lived in the house. It is currently the residence of Dr. Thornton Vandersall.

CORWIN HOUSE

One of several early Corwin houses on Long Island, this one in Aquebogue, in the eastern end of Long Island, shows off a fine gambrel roof and front porch with built-in benches and sidelights around the entrance doorway.

LANGHANS HOUSE

Huntington Town Historian, Rufus Langhans is the owner of this home on Chichester Road which was built in 1705 by Walt Whitman's father on part of the 500 acre farm of Nehemia Whitman, the poet's great grandfather. Some of the exterior authenticity has been lost in extensive remodeling, but the interior retains the original style of the house. Notice the monogram on the chimney and just below that, the date the house was built.

FIVE GATES

Once the 257-acre farm of John Rogers, this house on the north side of Half Hollows Road in Huntington, was built in 1732. The chimney in the center of the house allows for fireplaces back to back, to insure maximum heat penetration in the house. The present owners, the Dow family, are restoring the house to its original condition. The property also includes the remainder of a windmill built when the house was built.

RICH HOUSE

Mr. and Mrs. Chauncey Rich own this house at 269 Park Avenue in Huntington. It was built in 1842. The gable in the front elevation center and the porch that stretches across the entire front of the house give it individuality, as do the tiny windows above the first floor porch.

ELM COTTAGE

Built between 1840 and 1858 on Woolsey Street in Huntington, Elm Cottage is an example of Gothic Revival architecture. While its historical designation protects the house from alterations, new houses were built on the property around it, and the house is no longer visible from the road.

NORTHVILLE GRANGE HALL

Built as a church in 1831, this sturdy building on Sound Avenue also served as a school and a public meeting hall for the citizens of Northville, a tiny community whose only other nonresidential building was a store. The original pews are still in place, a reminder of its earlier purpose.

BARTOW HOUSE

This house was built in 1790 and later moved to its present site at 71 Arbutus Road, Greenlawn. The original location of the house is still unknown, but it is being investigated by the Huntington Historian, Rufus Langhans, who received a state grant in 1974 to conduct title searches on historical sites.

GREGORY HOUSE

This house on Sweet Hollow Road in Huntington was built in 1710 by the Oakley family. A later family, needing more room, added to the original structure. The house has been thoroughly restored and is owned by the Gregory family.

SANDS HOUSE

Captain John Sands was the master of a sailing packet, and traded up and down the east coast. In 1695 he built this house and its accompanying lighthouse in Sands Point, an area then known as Cow Neck. Situated on Middle Neck Road, the house has been well preserved and was in the possession of the Sands family until 1935.

RAYNHAM HALL

Built in Oyster Bay in the 1730s by Samuel Townsend, this house was one of the centers of Revolutionary War espionage. Townsend's son Robert, alias Culper, Jr., was a member of the Long Island Spy Ring. The house also quartered the British major, John André, who hid a message in the house about the plot to capture West Point. Robert's sister Sally found the message and sent it to her brother, thereby preventing a major disaster to the patriot forces.

OLD MANSE

This building was the residence for the rector of the Sweet Hollow Presbyterian Church. The church was built in 1828 and the rectory, at 152 Old Country Road, Melville, was built some years later.

CASE—KING HOUSE

This house was originally built in Peconic in 1747,
altered in 1840 and occupied by Lt. Moses Case
and Horace King. It was threatened with extinction
recently when the land was needed for commercial
use. William B. Smith of Southold bought the house
as well as a Gothic Revival accessory building and
some ancient boxwood plants, and moved it all to
North Road in Southold where he is restoring it
for use as an office. Handmade trim, old beams
and hardware were replaced, as were the plastered
ceilings and walls. Fireplaces and chimneys which
had to be taken apart during the transfer, were
rebuilt brick by brick.

ROSLYN GRIST MILL

When it was built in 1701, farmers came from miles around to process their grain and exchange gossip at the Grist Mill, owned at times by the Robinsons, Motts, and the Onderdonks. In 1850, Joseph Hicks bought the mill for his son Benjamin, who with his brothers, managed the mill for sixty-six years. In 1916, the youngest brother, Isaac, met Harold Godwin, grandson of William Cullen Bryant, and the two restored the mill and converted it into a tearoom and museum. It became a popular meeting place for actors, authors and artists.

POWELL HOUSE

Quaker Thomas Powell bought this house at 434 Park Avenue Huntington in 1663 from Richard Ogden who built it in 1654. An influential citizen, known for his diplomacy with the Indians, Powell held almost every civil office in existence. In 1668, when British officials in Huntington tried to collect taxes imposed by the Church of England, Powell fled to Farmingdale. The Powell house changed hands several times until John Bloomfield Jarvis was born there in 1794. He became one of the country's leading engineers of railroads, canals, and the Croton River Reservoir.

MATTITUCK OCTAGON HOUSE

This architectural curiosity was built in the late 1850's by Orson Squire Fowler, a phrenologist and architectural dreamer who wrote a book called *A Home For All* published in 1856. Fowler designed a similarly shaped house in Huntington for Ezra Prime. Both houses were considered quite sophisticated for their time when octagonal architecture enjoyed a vogue. The Mattituck house in located on the corner of Main Road and Love Lane in the center of town.

WALT WHITMAN BIRTHPLACE

The birthplace of Walt Whitman in the village of West Hills, town of Huntington, is one of America's major literary shrines. The preservation was made possible by a group of local citizens who saved it from destruction in 1957, and presented the house to the New York Historical Sites Commission.

The house was built in 1810, nine years before the poet's birth by his father, using the simple design and construction typical of the period when farmers were their own architects and engineers. The windows, framed in finely detailed molding, used twelve panes over eight, a style popular at the time.

Although the poet's family moved to Brooklyn while Whitman was a child, he spent his summers with his mother's parents, the VanVelsors, who owned a farm in nearby Cold Spring. Later, Whitman taught school in Smithtown, Babylon, Norwich and other Long Island towns. His educational theories were ahead of his time for unlike most schoolmasters, Whitman didn't believe in corporal punishment. Children could be best taught through love rather than fear, he insisted.

Whitman acquired ownership in 1838 of a local newspaper, the Long Islander, which is still thriving in Huntington.

Now a museum, the brown-shingled Whitman house contains family possessions along with the desk where the poet wrote his poems.

PRIME OCTAGON HOUSE

Similar to the Octagon House in Mattituck, this model on Prime Avenue in Huntington, was built for Ezra Prime, by the same architect, Orson Squire Fowler. The Klaber family lived in the house for many years and both husband and wife, interested in history and architecture, restored the house extensively.

ONDERDONK HOUSE

The Onderdonks were among the earliest Dutch settlers on Long Island, and they became prosperous merchants as well as respected civil servants. Horatio Gates Onderdonk, the son of Joseph Onderdonk and Dorothy Montfort, built this Doric style mansion in Manhasset in 1830.

This superb example of Greek Revival architecture almost fell to ruin when it was abandoned during the depression years, but was restored when residents of the area petitioned for its restoration.

OBADIAH WASHINGTON–VALENTINE HOUSE

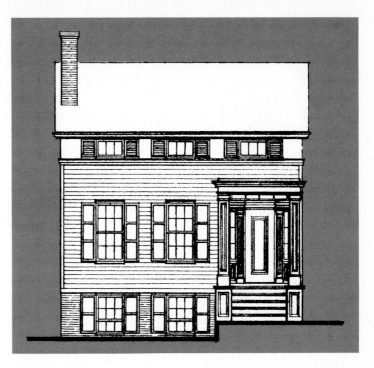

Built in Roslyn in 1835, this house is an example of the Greek Revival style popular during that period, giving way later in the century to the Federal style. Builder Thomas Wood suggested the Revival style with the tall basement well resembling the high podia of Greek Revival houses. The brick, in turn, rests on the rubble stone foundation below grade. The street facade, the principle one, has a fine Greek Revival doorway with sidelights and an over-the-door window. Richly molded single panel door and details could have been derived from architectural pattern books of the period.

LLOYD MANOR

The strategic location of this house in Lloyd's Neck overlooking Cold Spring Harbor, made it desirable to the British as a command post, and during the Revolutionary War, they built Fort Hill nearby. Some members of the Lloyd family were patriots and fled to Connecticut during the British occupation. Henry Lloyd, a loyalist remained but fled to England after the war when the Americans reclaimed his territory. Some years later, descendants reacquired the property and it was owned by the Lloyd family until recent times. The present owners are preserving the house which was built in 1722, and rebuilt in 1763. The fort, which the Americans were unable to capture during the Revolutionary War, has also been preserved.

SAG HARBOR CUSTOMS HOUSE

The first United States customs district for Long Island was established in 1788 at Sag Harbor, and the town thereby became the first customs port in New York State. By 1790, Sag Harbor had more tons of square-rigged vessels engaged in foreign commerce than did the city of New York. In the front garden of the customs house is a boxwood plant from Martha Washington's garden in Mount Vernon.

WEBB HOUSE

Originally built in Greenport and functioning as an inn under Constant Booth from 1740, this building was moved in 1810 to North Road and became the home of the Webb family. In 1955, George R. Latham bought the old house and moved it by barge to Village Lane in Orient where he restored, landscaped and furnished the house in its original style. It is now open to the public.

THE OLD HOUSE AT CUTCHOGUE

One of the oldest wooden houses in New York State, the house was built in Southold in 1649 by John Budd of England, a great grandson of the Earl of Warwick. The original four-room house was moved to Cutchogue in 1660 and given to Budd's daughter Anna on her marriage to Benjamin Horton, a carpenter. The house is designed in a fashion typical of the period with small windows and enormous fireplaces, one of which measures nine feet by five feet, showing the need of the early settlers for protection against the winter weather. The framing, stemming from English late medieval times, is of heavy timber, mortised and tenoned, secured by wooden pegs called treenails. The original walls were insulated with seaweed, and the interior finished with a mixture of oyster and clam shell plaster. The exterior sheathing is covered with narrow clapboards. The house is now the property of the Congregational Society of Cutchogue, and was restored to its original condition in 1949 for the Southold Tercentenary Celebration.

SAGTIKOS MANOR

This 42-room mansion is larger than most manor houses of its time. Overlooking Great South Bay in the village of Bay Shore, it was built in 1692 by Stephanus Van Cortlandt who was granted permission by the King to purchase

twelve hundred acres from the Indians who called the area "Saghtekoos," which meant "home of the snake that hisses." The white man called it Appletree Neck. Some years later, Jonathan Thompson bought the manor for $1200 for his son Isaac who later became a magistrate of the King. During the British occupation of Bay Shore in the Revolutionary War, Judge Thompson was forced to quarter 300 troops in his home. A soldier once took a shot at the judge while Thompson walked up the stairs carrying a candle; the soldier insisted the judge was going to signal the enemy. During a bout of drunken rowdiness, soldiers decided to hang the judge and dragged him by the neck to a stately tree outside. His pleas that they could not do this to the King's magistrate, finally saved him. During more peaceful times, Thompson had President George Washington as his guest. In the nineteenth century the manor became the property of the Gardiner family. Julia Gardiner married President John Tyler in 1844 and developed a reputation as one of the most flamboyant first ladies, even though Tyler's term had but nine months left after their marriage. In the 1960s Robert David Lion Gardiner, the last owner, deeded the manor and ten acres to Suffolk County. The Sagtikos Manor Historical Society operates the house as a museum and its rooms are filled with Indian relics, historical portraits, antique firearms, even the bullet hole in the staircase and the bed in which George Washington slept.

SHERWOOD JAYNE HOUSE

This saltbox house on Old Post Road in East Setauket, was built in 1730 by the son of William Jayne, a chaplain in Cromwell's army, who came to America in 1670. A wing was added in 1790. Howard C. Sherwood, founder of the Society for the Preservation of Long Island Antiquities, lived in the house for many years and furnished it with his collection of early Americana. The paneling in the west parlor is taken from an old parsonage in the village, and some of the furnishings are from an earlier home in Manhattan. Decorative wall painting adorns the parlor and east bedroom. Sherwood bequeathed the house to the society.

ROCK HALL

One of the finest Georgian-Colonial homes in the country, Rock Hall, in Lawrence, was presumably built in 1767. In that year John Cornell sold Josiah Martin 600 acres of land and everything on it. Martin, a wealthy man, enlarged and improved the property considerably. In 1824 Thomas Hewlett bought the property and it remained in the Hewlett family until 1948 when the house and three acres were given to the town of Hempstead. The house is maintained as a museum.

THOMPSON HOUSE

When the Rev. William Thompson arrived in this country in 1634, he founded one of Long Island's oldest and most illustrious families. Following five generations of judges, gunsmiths, doctors and farmers, Benjamin Thompson, in the sixth generation, made his mark as a historian for the island. His *History of Long Island* was first published in 1839. The brown shingled salt box on North Country Road in Setauket where he was born was built around 1700. It is now the headquarters of the Society for the Preservation of Long Island Antiquities and open to the public as a museum. The character of life in the house is reflected in the furnishings, including a quilt made from the wedding dress of Benjamin Thompson's mother.

SAMMIS HOUSE

On the list of historic Huntington homes is this old home of the John Sammis family. The 18th century Colonial on John Dave Lane, has been preserved in its original style and is now surrounded by a modern suburban development. The Sammis brothers were merchants in Huntington, and several businesses there still bear the name. John Dave Lane is named for John and David Sammis.

FLEET GOLDSMITH KENDRICK HOUSE

One of the oldest houses of the early settlers is the eighteenth century Georgian on New Suffolk Lane in Cutchogue. The Gambrel roof, typifying Dutch design, is unusual for the eastern end of the island since the Dutch mostly settled in the western areas.

JARED WADE HOUSE

Located in Sag Harbor, this Cape Cod is one-and-a-half stories with the twelve by twelve light sash so typical of the 18th century style. The front cornice with the five small brackets and the entrance are of the Federal style. The elliptical fanlight over the doorway serves as a window to light the upper floor. The doorway itself, with its sidelights and low horizontal transom form an unusual combination.

CLINTON ACADEMY

This school on Main Street in East Hampton was incorporated in 1787 and became the first academy to be chartered by the New York State Board of Regents. Construction of the building was begun in 1784 by the founder, the Rev. Dr. Samuel Buell, and it was named on completion after George Clinton, the first elected governor of New York and later Vice-President of the United States.

HAMPTON HOUSE

Renowned artist Nathan Rogers lived in this house in Bridgehampton until he died in 1844. Rogers, the son of John T. Rogers and grandson of Rev. James Brown was born in Bridgehampton of modest means. As a youth he went to work as an apprentice to an upstate shipbuilder. An accident to his knee forced him to resign and he took up the study of art under a Mr. Wood of New York City. Rogers became a leading miniature painter of his day. With his new affluence, he returned to Bridgehampton, built Hampton House and lived in it the rest of his life.

THE CUPOLA HOUSE

A cupola atop a Long Islander's house gave it a mark of distinction. This house built in Orient in 1862 is an example of the cupola style, and although not a very large house it does give the illusion of width. The front porch is finely detailed with "gingerbread" brackets.

SYLVESTER MANOR

This pre-Revolutionary house on Shelter Island is still owned by the descendants of Nathaniel and Grissell Sylvester, prominent Quakers. Shelter Island, so named because it offered a shelter to Quakers fleeing religious persecution, was purchased in the early 17th century by a group of sugar merchants. Sylvester was the only one who made the island his permanent home. This first Sylvester Manor was built in 1652 but a descendant, Brinley Sylvester, built the present day manor in 1735, incorporating parts of the original house. The manor includes a windmill, one of the few remaining in the country.

MANOR OF ST. GEORGE

In 1686 William "Tangier" Smith, formerly a page and civil servant to King Charles II emigrated to the aristocratic section of Long Island facing Great South Bay that is now

Mastic. Gradually building up an enormous estate, Smith petitioned the King who raised the estate to the Manor of St. George, the name by which it is still known. During the Revolutionary War the British erected a fort on the property. It became the scene of a famous battle and the fort was captured and destroyed by the American rebels. The Georgian style house along with 127 acres was given in 1954 to Suffolk County as a historical site by Eugenie Annie Tangier Smith, the last lineal descendant of the original William "Tangier" Smith who had thirteen children. Smith Point and Smith Point Bridge to Fire Island are named for the original family. The famous "Bull" Smith who founded Smithtown was a member of this family.

JARVIS FLEET HOUSE

The original portion of this Huntington house at
424 Park Avenue was built by Timothy Wood in
1653. In 1659 it was occupied by Richard Latting,
who was later banished from town for "turbulent
behavior." In 1702 Capt. William Jarvis, a whaler,
built the addition against the older cabin. The
front shingles are the original cypress shakes brought
from the West Indies. The house served at one
period as a general store and after the Revolutionary
War Samuel Fleet lived and kept the town post
office here. His son, Samuel, Jr., was a well known
educator and publisher.

GEORGE LATHAM HOUSE

The communities of Williston Park and East Williston owe their names to Henry Willis, an inventor
who had a large farm in the area known now as
Old Westbury. This house is the original pre-
Revolutionary homestead of Willis, who invented

and manufactured "East Boston Road Carts."
Because of a unique spring arrangement, these carts
were ideal for the rough roads of the time. George
Latham bought the old homestead and carefully
restored it.

MILLER PLACE LIBRARY

Built in 1834, this compact Federal style structure
originally served as a school for the children of
Miller Place. It is now a public library and a valuable witness of early Americana.

JOEL BARNUM SMITH HOUSE

This house on Godfrey Lane in Greenlawn was built between 1750 and 1780 by Joel Barnum Smith.

CONKLIN HOUSE

David and Sybil Conklin built this house in the mid 1700s and it remained in the Conklin family until 1911 when it was bequeathed to the Huntington Historical Society which uses it as headquarters and a museum for the public. Additions were added as the family grew to include nine children and the result is a fascinating fifteen-room house with no particular design. The Conklin furnishings on display include such curiosities as a long-handled toaster, a wooden apple peeler, a brick wall oven, a sausage grinder with wooden teeth and a revolving butter churn.

MAIN STREET, COLD SPRING HARBOR

The major part of Cold Spring Harbor has been declared a Historic District, including Main Street, in this picturesque three-hundred year old village, a thriving whaling town of yore. Construction of a mill dam in the eighteenth century is responsible for the three ponds which extend most of the length of this beautiful valley. Just west of the dams, George Washington paused while traveling in 1790. He shook hands with several townspeople engaged in "raising the rafter" for a school. A high proportion of landmarks from the late 1700s to the mid 1800s are found here.

BENJAMIN HOUSE

Time has taken its toll on this house, the birthplace of Simeon Benjamin, founder and benefactor of Elmira College, the first college for women in the country. The rear wing of the house in Southold was built in 1715 with the aid of local Indians; the front part was built in 1829. The Benjamin family had extensive land holdings in this area, which they purchased from the Indians in exchange for "a fat young heifer." The town of Riverhead plans to preserve the house as a historic landmark.

HALSEY HOUSE

It is claimed that this house in Southampton is one of the oldest saltbox frame houses in New York State. It was built in 1648 by Thomas Halsey and his wife. This type house, favored by the English, is identified by the lack of a porch. The saltbox always faced south no matter which way the road ran. It was usually two stories in front with a slanted roof and at the rear sometimes less than one story. Windows were few and small, since glass was an expensive commodity, and the three-foot cedar shingles were unpainted.

BEDLAM STREET, COLD SPRING HARBOR

"Bedlam" was the name given to a section of Main Street during the rowdy whaling years between 1836 and 1852. So many crew members of different nationalities filled the busy streets that someone said it was bedlam. And the name stuck.

A good whaling voyage usually lasted two or three years and netted each man $300 so when he was ashore after three years at sea, and with money in his pockets, he probably could do little else than create bedlam.

THE WHEELBARROW, COLD SPRING HARBOR

This is one of the typical shops on the Main Street in Cold Spring Harbor. The buildings retain no particular architectural distinction, and many have been altered for commercial use, but the whole is greater than the sum of its parts here. All the buildings are valuable components of a unique and especially characteristic area of regional as well as cultural significance.

SUYDAM HOUSE

Restoration has disclosed that the northwest corner room of the main structure of this house in Centerport was built first, a typical 17th century house with six-post frame. The house has four fireplaces and a beehive oven in which Nathan Hale was said to have been discovered hiding from the British after his undercover landing in Huntington Harbor. The patriot was disguised as a Dutch school teacher and hoped to smuggle information through the enemy lines.

EXITUS ACTA PROBAT

Washington

Early American Inns

WASHINGTON MANOR

This famous Roslyn restaurant was built in 1753 and was the home of Henry Onderdonk who owned the nearby Grist Mill and Paper Mill. During the Revolutionary War Onderdonk was forced to play host to British troops, but it was a later, more gracious guest, who gave the place its name. In 1790 President George Washington stopped at Onderdonk's house during his tour of Long Island. He was so impressed with Onderdonk's hospitality that he made note of it in his journal.

LA GRANGE INN

One of Long Island's landmarks, the La Grange Inn on Montauk Highway in Babylon dates back to the early 18th century. Though there have been different inkeepers, the inn has been in continuous operation since colonial times.

TOWNSEND MANOR INN

The portico and detail of the Townsend Manor Inn in Greenport are excellent examples of the Greek Revival style. Built in 1835, the inn has been remarkably well kept. The usual round columns of the style are replaced here by square piers. Greenport was a major resort area in the 19th century, competing only with Southampton.

MILLERIDGE INN

Probably the most well known of all Colonial inns is this one on Route 106 in Jericho. The Milleridge Inn was built in 1676 and the original structure is still in use. Additions have been made and also some alterations to facilitate the restaurant, but the atmosphere is about as authentic as anyone could want.

39

PEACE AND PLENTY INN
TAP ROOM

It's uncertain when the old Chichester Inn at 197 Chichester Road in West Hills was established, but the building dates back as far as 1690. This legendary watering spot on the main road was a stopover for stage coaches from New York. James Chichester, one of the earliest proprietors was "elected" innkeeper for the town and reelected annually. Generations of Chichesters followed suit. Early American pewter utensils are displayed on the shelves in the tap room.

Places of Worship

OLD FIRST CHURCH

The town of Huntington was settled in 1643, and when the first settlers, intensely religious, purchased the land from the Matinecock Indians, there was no church and no time to build one. For twelve years they and their families, mostly Congregationalists, gathered for services in each other's homes.

At last, in 1665, they raised their first church, a crude wooden structure with bare floors, a rough-hewn pulpit and pews, and oil paper for window glass. Each parishioner brought along his own hot stove and bricks to use as foot-warmers.

Rigorous rules provided that the men would sit on one side; the women on the other. Slaves and children were assigned to the balcony. This primary little church was torn down in 1715 so that a new, larger church could be built. The second might still be standing, but during the Revolutionary War, British troops tore down the church and used the wood to build Fort Golgotha in the middle of the burying ground. Tombstones ripped from the ground were used to make fireplaces and ovens in the fort.

The Rector, Reverend Prime, an implacable foe of the British, died in 1779 and the British Colonel Thompson pitched his tent so that whenever he left it, he would be trodding on the grave of that "damned rebel."

When the war ended, the parishioners, now Presbyterians, again collected money and in 1784 built the present church. It wasn't really finished until 1789 when Admiral Digby returned the bell cast in 1715 which the British had stolen for one of their frigates. It was so cracked that it had to be recast, but the old bell was once more mounted high in the tower.

The shingles are hand finished and held in place by handmade nails, all protected by layers of white paint. The framing shows the influence of shipwrights so often revealed in shore communities.

ST. GEORGE EPISCOPAL CHURCH

The weather vane atop this historic church in Hempstead has sixteen bullet holes
put there during the Revolutionary War by British soldiers holding target practice.
The clock in the tower was built in 1852, two years before Big Ben in London
was built, and it is a landmark on Front Street. The present church was built in
1822, but previous buildings of the congregation date back to 1648. It is considered one of the finest examples of Georgian architecture in America.

EAST NASSAU TEMPLE

The tablets of the Ten Commandments present an inter-
esting treatment of the stained glass windows of the East
Nassau Temple. This is the front facade on South Oyster
Bay Road in Syosset.

SETAUKET PRESBYTERIAN CHURCH

The First Presbyterian Church of
Brookhaven, in Setauket, was
considered the fashionable church
of the Brookhaven area. Although
many of the wealthy land-
owners lived on the south shore
they returned to Setauket to
attend services. The first structure was a crude wooden building,
twenty eight feet square. It stood
until 1715 when it was replaced
by a larger more comfortable
one. The present building was
erected in 1811.

SMITHTOWN PRESBYTERIAN CHURCH

The Rev. Daniel Taylor was the first minister of this church built in 1712 at the intersection of Moriches Road and Nissequogue River Road on land donated by the children of Richard Smith. In 1750, the building was dismantled and moved to its present site in The Village of the Branch. In 1827, George Curtis was paid $825 to rebuild the church. Its style is a mixture of many church styles popular then, Federal, Greek Revival and Gothic.

SWEET HOLLOW PRESBYTERIAN CHURCH

The Reverend William Schenck was the first pastor of the Sweet Hollow Presbyterian Church in Melville, built in 1828. It is on Old Country Road near Sweet Hollow Road.

SOUTHOLD UNIVERSALIST CHURCH

Early in the nineteenth century architects began experimenting with style, and this church built in 1837 is the result of an eclectic blend put together under the Gothic heading by architect W. D. Cochran. The pointed windows, battlemented tower, and tall belfry suggest Gothic style. But the large elliptical window on the front elevation, the corner pilasters, are Federal. There is a suggestion of Greek Revival in the lower roof pitch and the cornices. The church is famous among architects because it has the only Gothic Palladian window in existence.

OLD SOUTH HAVEN PRESBYTERIAN CHURCH

Though this church was incorporated in 1745, the present building, which has been moved to South Country Road in Brookhaven village, was not built until 1828.

BELLPORT METHODIST CHURCH

Formerly a meeting place for a Presbyterian Parish, the Methodist Church of Bellport was built in 1850. Its Doric pilasters, full entablature and relatively low pitched roof identify the typical Greek Revival style. The square belfry with octagonal spire athwart the roof ridge indicates its purpose as a church. The Corinthian pilaster capitals behind the pulpit are stock trim made of papier-maché by a manufacturer of architectural ornaments.

WHALERS' PRESBYTERIAN CHURCH

The First Presbyterian Church, in Sag Harbor, known as the Whalers' Church was built in 1843. The architect was Minard Lafener. The tall steeple served as a landfall for scores of whaling ships whose home port was Sag Harbor.

MT. SINAI CONGREGATIONAL CHURCH

This church built some time before 1835 is on a gently sloping elevation overlooking Mt. Sinai harbor and Mt. Misery Point. Enhanced by the adjacent Hopkins-Madsen preservation, the classic white shingled church is still used for religious services. It is located on North Country Road.

MATTITUCK CHURCH

One of the earlier Presbyterian churches on this site in Mattituck burned and the present building was erected in 1853 and enlarged in 1871. Many of the headstones in the graveyard date back to the 1700s.

NEW VILLAGE CONGREGATIONAL CHURCH

When this church was built in 1815, Lake Grove was known as New Village. The lower windows, now paneless, are boarded up with plywood. This church is no longer in use since the congregation built a new church several blocks east. The town of Brookhaven is reportedly planning to restore the old building which is located near the huge Smithaven Shopping Mall.

MANETTO HILL METHODIST CHURCH

Built in 1853 in Plainview, this church was moved recently to Old Bethpage as part of a pre-Civil War farm restoration.

ST. GEORGE'S PARISH HOUSE

Built in the late 1700s, this Georgian building annexed St. George's Church in Hempstead. The Dutch roof, used extensively during that time, is making a comeback in modern home design. This roof has equal slopes which are truncated, and it has dormer windows on each side.

UNIVERSALIST CHURCH

The Huntington Chapter of the Daughters of the Revolution have used this church for their headquarters since 1914. Built in 1837 as a house of worship for the Universalist Society, the church at 9 Nassau Road, was shared with other denominations.

FRIENDS MEETING HOUSE

The Society of Friends, more commonly called Quakers, were among the earliest religious groups to settle here. Though the British rule discriminated against Friends, early settlers of other faiths fought for freedom of worship and badgered the British into allowing Friends their right to congregate. The utter simplicity of their house of worship typifies their religion. This house in Old Westbury is similar to many others on the island, where a congregation of Friends would gather in silence on hard benches in the large one room building.

ST. JAMES EPISCOPAL CHURCH

A congregation of Episcopalians who had been traveling to
Caroline Church in Setauket for their services were finally
able to build their own church in 1853, and hired noted
architect Richard Upjohn. Soon after the church was built,
a post office was established under the name St. James. The
name soon spread and the village of St. James was born.
The church's tall square tower, high roof, lancet windows
and marked feeling of verticality are typical of the Gothic
Revival style. The stained glass window of the nave was
designed by Louis Comfort Tiffany, of Oyster Bay, noted
art noveau decorative designer of his day, and the creator of
Tiffany favrile glass.

TRINITY EVANGELICAL LUTHERAN CHURCH

Built more than 100 years later, in 1964, this Rocky Point church
designed by Edwin Slater, is a striking example of contemporary
architecture. Though many churches of today are still built in
the traditional forms, this one is a striking example of new thinking
in church design while the feeling of reverance is still maintained.
Trinity Evangelical Lutheran Church is located on Route 25A.

FIRST CHURCH OF CHRIST SCIENTIST

CHRISTIAN SCIENCE CHURCH, HUNTINGTON

The First Church of Christ Scientist is an interesting
addition to the town of Huntington's architectural
style. The arcade to the director's room adds to its
charm.

ST. JOHN'S EPISCOPAL CHURCH

Sixty-eight families contributed toward the cost of this church built in 1831 in Cold Spring Harbor on land purchased for $300. The salary for the first rector, Isaac Sherwood, and the sexton Simon Rice, came from pew rentals which sometimes amounted to $25 per family for a two year period. The sexton, who received $20 plus a pew for his services, augmented his income by digging graves at $1.75 apiece. In 1839 a rectory was acquired, and in 1862, a chancel added. The church, on the south side of Route 25A, was remodeled in the 1880s.

GARDEN CITY CATHEDRAL

Also known as the Cathedral of the Incarnation, this magnificent church was built by the widow of Alexander T. Stewart in his memory. A successful New York merchant, Stewart was the founder of Garden City. In 1869 he bought seven thousand acres of land from the town of Hempstead at $55 an acre and laid it out in broad avenues, brought in his own spur of the Long Island railroad, and started building houses for select upper middle class population. As a result, Garden City today is one of the best planned communities in the country. Following Stewart's death in 1876, his widow began the construction of the cathedral which took seven years to complete.

There is a legend that Stewart's body was stolen from the graveyard and held for ransom. When the ransom was paid a body was returned, but no one knew for sure it was Stewart's. In any case, the remains were sealed in the still unfinished cathedral in a crypt that was wired so that any tampering would set off the church bells.

METHODIST CHURCH OF HEMPSTEAD

The one hundred sixty foot spire on the Methodist Church on Front Street in Hempstead has been a landmark ever since it was built in 1855.

57

NEWTOWN REFORMED CHURCH

In 1731, with volunteer labor, work was begun on
the original Dutch Reformed church in Newtown,
now known as Elmhurst. The octagonal building
was finished two years later. The congregation
had great difficulty obtaining a minister, and finally
in 1739, they combined with three other Dutch
Reformed congregations to hire a minister who
would serve all four parishes. This arrangement
lasted until 1802. During the Revolutionary War,
the minister, an ardent supporter of the American
colonists, was forced to flee when the British
occupied Long Island and used the Newtown Church
as an ammunition storehouse. The language of the
church was Dutch until 1802 when it became bi-
lingual. In 1831 the original structure was taken
down and using the original cornerstone, the present
building was erected.

Lighthouses and Towers

EATON'S NECK LIGHT

The second oldest lighthouse on Long Island, the Eaton's Neck
Light was built in 1798. Its designer was John J. McComb, Jr.,
the architect responsible for New York's City Hall. McComb
was paid $9,750 for his work on the lighthouse which was badly
needed because of a hazardous off shore reef said to be responsible for more shipwrecks than any other point on the north
shore. In a severe storm on April 11, 1883, four schooners were
wrecked on the rocks here in one day. Coast Guardsmen stationed
at Eaton's Neck were able to save all crew members, avoiding
further tragedy. Today radio gear at this light controls five
other lighthouses from Throgs Neck to Stratford Shoals in
Connecticut.

THE CAMPANILE, JONES BEACH

This tower at Jones Beach State Park houses the
water tank for part of the popular recreation center.
The tower, and several other buildings in the park
were built in the thirties with brick, granite and
limestone.

RIENT POINT LIGHT

ilt on Oyster Pond Reef in the late 1800s, a
ree-man crew operated this light until it was auto-
ated in 1958. The red beacon atop the sixty-
ur foot tower is visible for miles.

EXECUTION ROCK LIGHTHOUSE

A dangerous reef in the middle of the Long Island Sound, between Port Washington and New Rochelle, made construction of this lighthouse imperative, and it was completed in 1850. A breakwater was added to protect ships which service the lighthouse. The grim name of the site is taken from the executions which were carried out here during the Revolutionary War.

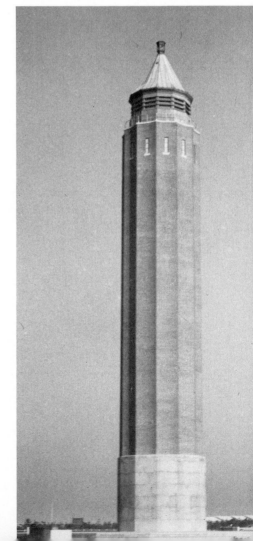

CAMPANILE, ROBERT MOSES STATE PARK

This park was named for the man who saw Long Island as a playground for New Yorkers, Robert Moses, the state's Parks Commissioner. The popularity of Jones Beach, another Moses creation, spurred the opening of this second facility on the island's south shore, on Fire Island, southeast of Babylon.

EISENHOWER PARK MEMORIAL

The eight sides of this Nassau County Veterans Memorial mark the eight wars the United States has fought to insure freedom. Designed by Arnold Rinaldi, the structure houses a 111 bell carillon which can be heard for a mile around Eisenhower Park. The interior niches of the memorial are marble and the exterior is made of brick, limestone and granite.

MONTAUK LIGHT

Located on the eastern tip of Long Island, the Montauk Light has been guiding mariners for 178 years. The one hundred eight foot tower was recently refurbished by the Coast Guard, and has a new two-and-one-half million candlepower lamp, visible for nineteen miles. The beacon, one of the most important on the east coast, was authorized for construction by George Washington in 1796, when whale oil was the fuel that lighted the lamp. The ocean has eroded one hundred feet of the land in front of the light since the tower was erected.

FIRE ISLAND LIGHT

The first lighthouse was built on Fire Island in 1826 and consisted of eighteen lamps, with fifteen reflectors, producing a white flash every minute-and-a-half. In 1842 the light was refitted with bigger and better reflectors. The present light was built in 1858, and has been modernized since then. The tower is 150 feet high and the light can be seen a distance of nineteen nautical miles in clear weather.

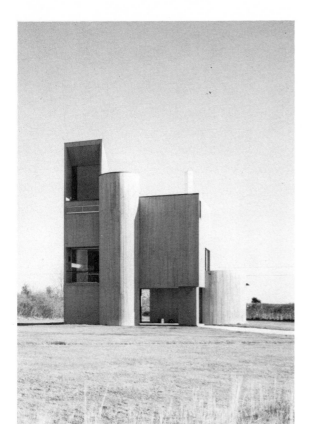

Residences

WITKIN HOUSE

East end beaches are dotted with summer houses
of all variety. This one was designed by Andrew
Geller, demonstrating an attempt for the spectacular.

HANSON HOUSE

The butterfly roof, like this one on the Hanson
family home in Huntington, is a popular example
of contemporary architecture. Vertical siding, fine
stonework and expanses of wide glass blend the
structure into its setting, creating a harmony of
architecture and nature.

GWATHMEY HOUSE

This contemporary house and studio was built for
the artist Robert Gwathmey in 1965 by his son,
an architect with Gwathmey and Henderson.
Vertical siding and broken roof lines are among the
characteristics of this unique style. The stark landscape of sand on the island's east end demands
simplicity of design.

HOUSE BY THE SEA

Gwathmey and Henderson were the architects for
this dramatic contemporary beach house, in its
setting of soft sand dunes and waving beach grass.
The vertical sheathing, and long bridge-way to the
top of the dunes, suggest an "International" style.

BRECKNOCK HALL

Scottish masons were imported
to do the stonework on this
Greenport estate built for whaling magnate David Gelston
Floyd in 1857. Stone was a
material not readily available
on the island at the time, and its
use here attests to Floyd's
affluence.

CEDARMERE

In 1843, William Cullen Bryant became one of Long Island's first commuters. Bryant the editor loved the activity and clamor of metropolitan New York, but Bryant the poet longed for peace and rural beauty. Answering a classified advertisement, he found his suburban home in Roslyn, an old fashioned house built in 1787. Bryant remodeled the old house, making it a large comfortable home, surrounded by gardens and orchards sloping down to the water's edge. He named his home Cedarmere, after the native cedar trees which grew there. Elizabeth L. Godwin, a great granddaughter of the poet was the last resident of Cedarmere.

BREESE HOUSE

Originally a farmhouse built by Capt. D. R. Drake in 1858, this stately colonial mansion on Hill St. in Southampton was purchased in the 1890s by James Breese. Architect Sanford White was hired by Breese to remodel and alterations made the farmhouse hardly recognizable. White added a music room in 1906. The ballroom's linen-fold paneling and wooden coffered ceiling are in the European style. Until recently the building housed the Nyack School for Boys.

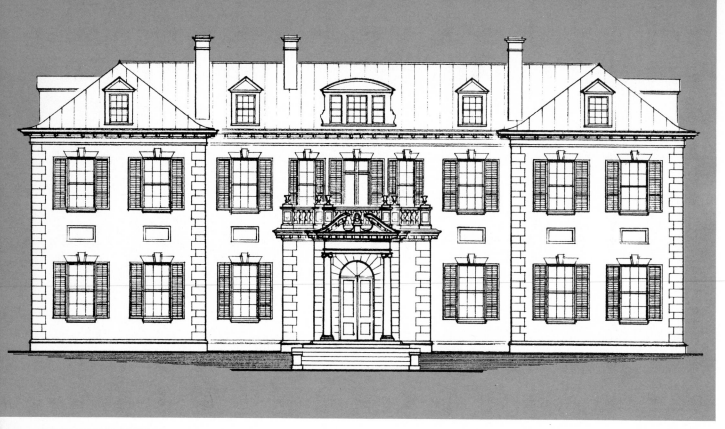

BRYCE RESIDENCE

This Gold Coast mansion in Roslyn was built in 1893 by Lloyd Bryce, lawyer, author, and owner of the *North American Review.* Ogden Codman, Jr. was the architect. After Bryce's death, the new owner, Childs Frick, son of one of the founders of U.S. Steel, had alterations done by Sir Charles Allom, of Murphy and Dana. In 1969 Nassau County purchased the estate for use as a nature preserve.

GARDINER'S ISLAND

Lion Gardiner, an English subject, was granted an island in Long Island Sound in 1639, and the Gardiner family has occupied it ever since. Today, Robert David Lion Gardiner, 17th Lord of the Manor, lives there. The first Gardiner reportedly paid to the Indians, one large black dog, one gun, some powder and shot and a few blankets for use of the island. Today, the property tax alone on Gardiner's Island is $1000 a day. The early settlers had Lion Gardiner to thank for the peaceful relations with the Indians. Gardiner was a life-long friend of Wyandanch, Chief of the Montauks.

OLD WESTBURY GARDENS

Taking its name from the area, this baronial
mansion was originally built for Wall St. magnate
John S. Phipps and his wife. "Mike" Phipps, a later
generation, was an internationally known polo
player. The Old Westbury house, its out-buildings
and gardens have been preserved in their complete
magnificence. The formal gardens are filled with
pools, statuary, the famed Temple of Love, and
other accessories of a garden designed in the grand
manner. The gardens have been used as settings for
soap operas, television commercials and photographs.
The gardens were designed to blend unobtrusively
with the surrounding fields and meadows and other
natural features. The house itself is furnished with
pictures and furniture of the English Georgian period.
An endowment keeps the gardens preserved and open
for the public view.

COE ESTATE

William R. Coe emigrated from England as a penniless teenager and went to work in New York City as an office boy. He eventually made a fortune in the insurance business, and spent part of that fortune on his country house in Oyster Bay. To embellish this sixty-room English tudor style mansion, Coe bought a pair of entrance gates which were made in the eighteenth century in England. Coe's purchase of the gates and their removal caused considerable uproar in official and unofficial places in Britain. The gates still stand on the Chicken Valley Rd. entrance to the estate. Coe was an avid collector of plants and shrubs from all over the world and his gardens are a living tribute to his enthusiasm. The Coe family set aside certain days of the week, while they were still living there, to allow the public to visit their gardens and greenhouses. They are still open to the public. Later the State acquired the land for its university chain, and today botany and horticulture students have one of the most beautiful academic settings in New York. Garden club meetings, as well as gardening seminars and workshops for the public are frequently held at the estate.

CASTRO HOUSE

This house in Lloyd Harbor is the former Milbank Estate, built during the opulent era of the twenties. Its present occupants are the Castro family of Castro Convertible fame.

MATINECOCK FARM

In 1678 John Underhill, Jr., son of the famous Capt. John Underhill, built what is
now known as Matinecock Farm in Locust
Valley, purchasing the land from his father-
in-law, Matthew Prior, who held the land
under an Indian deed. The original house
was expanded shortly after 1756 and in 1820
another John Underhill built an adjacent
water powered woolen mill on Corn Creek,
and established a mixed farming and industrial complex. The property remained in the
Underhill family until about 1903 and in
1957 John W. Mackay, a decendant of Capt.
John Underhill, purchased the entire set of
buildings, as well as about twenty five acres
of the original Underhill property, and
moved these to a new site not far from their
original setting on Mill Neck Creek. The
buildings are now operated as a small farm,
including the original windmill and a marsh
preserve for wild waterfowl and songbirds.

Clubs and Recreation

JONES BEACH

The longtime dream of State Parks Commissioner Robert Moses, Jones Beach State Park, opened in 1929. It is one of the major recreational areas near metropolitan New York with pools, cabanas, restaurants, amusement facilities and miles of ocean beach. It was named for Thomas Jones who owned over 7,000 acres of marsh land and ocean front during the late seventeenth and early eighteenth centuries.

JONES BEACH THEATRE

Off Broadway theatre is less than an hour's drive from New York City and it's well worth the trip to see a musical show like The *King and I,* or *South Pacific* performed on this outdoor theatre-in-the-round. The judicious use of floating scenery, barges, water sprays and lights make any performance an extravaganza here. A day in the Jones Beach surf followed by an evening at the theatre, make a trip to Jones Beach more like a mini-vacation. Even in winter the beach, especially the boardwalk at left, is a popular spot for cyclists, joggers and just plain strollers.

79

CHARTER OAKS COUNTRY CLUB

A private club has recently taken over the former estate of the Brewster family on Northern Boulevard in Muttontown. The interiors, with magnificent paneling, elaborate ceilings, and numerous fireplaces, offer luxurious accomodations for Charter Oaks's members. Only minimal alterations were required for the addition of locker rooms and showers. The club also has an eighteen hole championship golf course.

THE VILLAS

Architect Richard Foster won a 1973 award from the Long Island Association of Commerce and Industry for this innovative approach to housing. The Villas, part of the Montauk Golf and Racquet Club, is a condominium development. Each series of buildings are strung together, donut style, and the circular arrangement gives occupants a view of the golfing area, while hiding automobiles from open sight.

EISENHOWER PARK CLUBHOUSE

Available for the residents of Nassau County, Eisenhower Park was formerly known as Salisbury park because of its location in Salisbury. The name was changed after President Eisenhower's death. The park contains three golf courses (rather flat because the area is part of the Hempstead Plains), playgrounds, a lake, picnic areas, a roller skating rink, a museum and an ancient locomotive that children may climb aboard.

BETHPAGE STATE PARK CLUBHOUSE

This park is open to all New York State residents. It has three 18-hole golf courses, as well as bridle paths, picnic area, etc. A polo field is used in season, with grandstands for spectators of this fast footed sport, very popular on Long Island during the Gold Coast era.

HECKSCHER PARK

This public park in Huntington was named for August Heckscher who made the park as well as an art museum a gift to the town in 1917. The park includes tennis courts and athletic fields as well as playgrounds. Once the Prime Farm, the park includes an old trout pond built as a dam by the Prime Thimble factory to impound the water from Meeting House Brook as a source of power.

SMITHTOWN MASONIC TEMPLE

Architects Viemeister and McBurney designed this twentieth century building in keeping with the style of surrounding Colonial structures.

CENTERPORT HARBOR EAST

. . . are raised and borne
By that great current in its onward sweep,
Wandering and rippling with caressing waves
Around green islands. . .
    from William Cullen Bryant's "The Flood of Years"

HUNTINGTON YACHT CLUB

The original club house of the Huntington Yacht Club was built at the harbor around 1880. It burned down in 1914 but was soon replaced by another building. The club provides boating facilities for members including tender services, docking, fuel. A pool and restaurant complete the picture. In winter, members enjoy "frost bite sailing" in the harbor.

ECHO PARK POOL COMPLEX

On Nassau Blvd. in West Hempstead, this recreation facility designed by Keith Hibner, won the 1973 silver award from the Long Island Association of Commerce and Industry.

Long Island from the Air

MONTAUK POINT

Jutting 125 miles out into the Atlantic, Montauk Point intercepts the path of game fish migrating along the Atlantic seacoast and world records for game catches have kept fishermen coming to Montauk Point after "the big one." In the seventeenth century, an agreement between the Montauk Indians and the settlers made the area a huge cattle range. During Prohibition, Montauk was an infamous drop-off point for rum runners, and in 1925, two hundred thousand dollars worth of bootleg liquor was unearthed there. The action of its colorful history contrasts with its serene rolling hills and sand dunes, reminiscent of the moors of Scotland.

NAVY-GRUMMAN AIRPORT

When it felt the need for another airfield on Long
Island, the United States Navy bought up several
thousand acres of potato fields in Calverton. Later,
the Navy collaborated with Grumman Aircraft Engineering Corporation to share use of the facility.
Grumman builds the planes and the Navy flies them.
The barbed wired complex stretches for miles along
the northeastern shore.

BAITING HOLLOW

This little village on the Long Island Sound has miles of beach with high bluffs and undisturbed woodlands. Fields of farm lands stretch out toward the Atlantic. The stream in the lower left foreground originates in a deep hollow or valley, from which this area draws its name.

BELMONT PARK

This famous race track, built in 1905, is the scene of "The Belmont," part of thoroughbred racing's Triple Crown event.

The track is located off Hempstead Turnpike on the flat Hempstead Plains of old. It was named for August Belmont, a legendary dean of flat racing. Nearby is the site of the first racetrack in the American colonies, set out along the Hempstead Plains in 1665.

When you think of the crowds that jam the parkways now to get to the track, it's hard to believe this notice that appeared in the New York Gazette on June 4, 1750: "A great Horse Race was run off at Hempstead Plains for a considerable wager which engaged the attention of so many in the city that upward of seventy chairs and chaises were carried over the ferry from thence, and a far greater number of horses!"

93

REPUBLIC AVIATION

At one time the second largest Long Island employer, Republic Aviation was famous for the Republic Thunderbolts, fighter planes used in World War II. The manufacturing plant and airport in Farmingdale are shown here. Republic is a division of the Fairchild Hiller Corporation. Because they made so many jobs available, Republic and Grumman greatly influenced the population boom on Long Island in the forties and fifties. The field known as Republic Airport is now a major satellite of the main New York airports. It is a unit of the Metropolitan Transit Authority.

ROOSEVELT RACEWAY

This half-mile harness racing track was built in Westbury in 1940 with a capacity for fifty-five thousand spectators. Nine races are held each evening during the harness racing seasons, usually two-month stretches in fall, winter, and spring. The highlight of the year is the annual International Stakes.

LEVITTOWN

This suburban development of low cost 2-bedroom homes built on a large tract of farm land in Hempstead Township 27 miles from New York City, started a revolution in mass produced housing for the working classes, and the suburban push across the county began. The development, named after its initiator, Levitt and Sons, provided homes for thousands of World War II veterans and their families with government financed mortgages and set a precedent in the home building industry, which implemented this successful 'experiment' across the country. Today, more than 25 years later, the houses built exactly alike, have taken on individual identities through the changes of a generation.

PORT WASHINGTON

Less than 20 miles from Manhattan, the bedroom community of Port Washington is a delightfully rural village on Manhasset Bay. It offers New Yorkers all the amenities of semi-rural living with only a 45-minute railroad trip to midtown Manhattan.

Old Bethpage

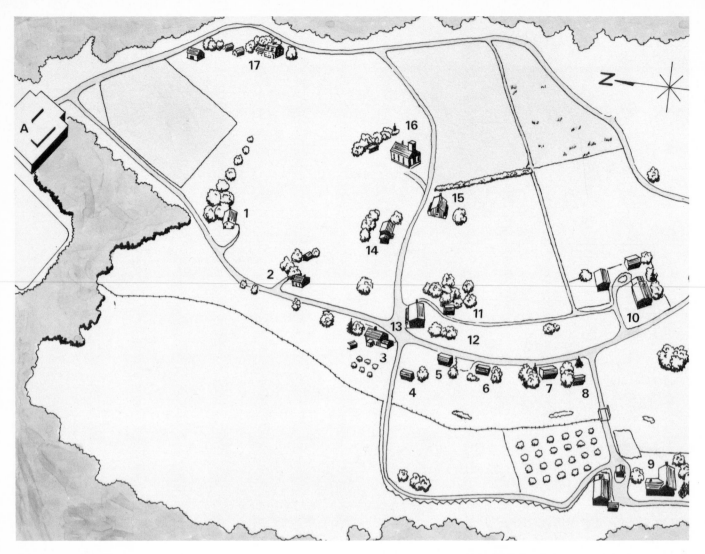

Map of Old Bethpage

A. Reception Center
1. Schenck House
2. Conklin House
3. Layton Store-House
4. Prime Storage Building
5. Luyster Store
6. Bach Blacksmith Shop
7. Cooper House
8. Rest Rooms
9. Powell Farm
10. Williams House and Carpentry Shop
11. Rest Rooms
12. Lawrence House
13. Noon Inn
14. Kirby House
15. Potter House
16. Manetto Hill Church
17. Hewlett Farm

OLD BETHPAGE

Nestled in a hidden valley in eastern Nassau County, Old Bethpage village depicts a typical rural Long Island village of the generation before the Civil War. Several historic homes, shops and farms have been moved from other parts of Long Island to create this restoration.

The buildings are furnished as they were long ago, and for a nominal admission charge, a visitor can step back in time. The village is a working restoration, and one can buy a glass of birch beer in the barroom, watch a farmer milk a cow, or see what's on the shelves at the general store.

POTTER HOUSE AND MANETTO HILL CHURC

The John L. Potter house, built in 1860 was move from its original site in Great Neck. The Manetto Hill Church, built in 1857 for the Methodist congregation was moved from Plainview.

LAYTON STORE AND HOUSE

John M. Layton was the storekeeper in this building erected in East Norwich in 1865. His family
had living quarters in the back of the building.

COOPER HOUSE

Peter Cooper, the inventor, built this house for his
family in 1815 in Hempstead.

POWELL FARM

This farm, built in 1850 by Richard S. Powell, is on its original site. The barns were moved from the Underhill farm in Syosset.

NOON INN

John H. Noon built his inn and residence in East Meadow in 1850.

WILLIAMS HOUSE AND CARPENTRY SHOP

Carpenter Henry R. Williams built this combination home
and place of business in New Hyde Park around 1850. The
barn is from the Daniel Underhill Farm in Jericho.

KIRBY HOUSE

A Hempstead tailor, Richard D. Kirby built this house
in 1840.

Educational Facilities

SUNQUAM ELEMENTARY SCHOOL

Part of the Half Hollow Hills school district in Melville,
this elementary school was designed by Daniel
Perry, who is responsible for many other Long Island
school designs. This one-story building was designed
to receive maximum sunlight and yet retain the inti-
macy of the one-room schoolhouse.

AMITYVILLE PUBLIC LIBRARY

A 1973 winner of an award from the Long Island
Association of Commerce and Industry, this public
library was designed by Bentel and Bentel who used
a refreshing simplicity with an adventurous combination of forms.

ADELPHI UNIVERSITY

This liberal arts college was founded in Brooklyn in 1896 as Adelphi Academy and Adelphi College. In 1929, the college moved to its present site in Garden City. It was recently granted university status by New York State. Keeping pace with the space age, Adelphi has built into the traditional liberal arts curriculum advanced programs in engineering and chemistry housed in the new science building above. Another recent addition is the students center, below.

ERASMUS HALL HIGH SCHOOL

This school, which developed a reputation for excellent scholarship, was founded in the Flatbush section of Brooklyn in 1786 as a boys' academy. The original academy is now in the center of the school's five-acre campus, completely surrounded by later buildings.

BROOKHAVEN NATIONAL LABORATORIES

This giant Federal installation located in the middle of Suffolk County has become one of the outstanding centers for atomic research in the world. Of particular importance are the extensive biological laboratories used to investigate the possible harmful affects of atomic radiation and fallout on living organisms, and also the beneficial uses to which atomic science can be put. Marcel Breuer drew up the master plan for the huge complex. The lecture hall and cafeteria buildings shown here were designed by Max O. Urbahn Associates in 1966, with concern for the psychological effect of space upon its occupants. Slanting walls, interestingly formed windows and skylights give the cafeteria an atmosphere of relief after the intense concentration of the lecture hall.

SMITHTOWN HIGH SCHOOL WEST

Lothrop Associates, architects, won the gold medal
for architectural excellence from the Long Island
Association of Commerce and Industry for this
contemporary brick and glass structure.

PARRISH ART MUSEUM

This building with a neat garden all around
it was given to the town of Southampton in
1897 by Samuel L. Parrish, a long time summer resident. In 1903 an addition was built
by James C. Parrish to be used as a lecture
hall and theatre. The museum on Jobs Lane,
open only in the summer, has an extensive
collection of reproductions of Greek and
Roman statues, and many well known
artists are exhibited here.

WHALING MUSEUM

One of two whaling museums on Long Island, this one in Cold Spring Harbor was founded in 1942 by Dr. Charles B. Davenport, a scientist, and Dr. Robert Cushman Murphy who sailed aboard the whaling brig *Daisy*. The museum has a full size whale boat from the *Daisy* which was built in Setauket and in use until 1913. There is also a try-pot used to boil whale blubber to make oil, a seven-foot ivory whale tusk, the skeletal remains of a killer whale as well as whaling tools and a large collection of scrimshaw.

STATE UNIVERSITY AT STONY BROOK

A considerable number of architects have designed this
sprawling multi-building campus, part of the New York
State University system, and one of the major centers
of learning on the east coast. The contemporary design
of light textured concrete shown here is used as a lecture hall. A circular multi-level medical science center
completed the complex in 1974, providing an astonish-
ing contrast of contemporary architecture with the
colonial restorations in the nearby village of Stony Brook.

DOWLING COLLEGE

This former 110-room mansion of William K. Vanderbilt is the home of Dowling College, a private institution in Oakdale, at the foot of the Connetquot River. The massive red brick, sandstone and marble mansion serves as the nucleus for the college. A fire in 1974 destroyed part of the interior and funds are being raised for its restoration. Designed in 1876 by R. H. Hunt, a leading architect of the time, the building is situated on 900 acres. Named "Idle Hour" for Vanderbilt and his young wife, Alva, a southern belle, the estate became the steppingstone for New York's elite "400." There were other buildings including an indoor tennis house, greenhouses, two gate houses, a tea house, carriage houses and stables. The college was founded as the Suffolk branch of Adelphi University and in 1965 became an independent school named for its benefactor and art patron, Robert W. Dowling.

POST COLLEGE LIBRARY

The dome of the C.W. Post College Library is the focal point of this campus in Old Brookville. The college was established in 1954 as a branch of Long Island University, on the former estate of Charles William Post, and named in his memory. The college's newer buildings, including dormitories, an auditorium and a science building have been carefully designed to blend with the traditional architecture of the era. The library has one of the largest collections on Long Island.

THE VANDERBILT MUSEUM

Used now as a Marine Museum, this estate at Center-port was built in the twenties as a summer home for William K. Vanderbilt II. The house is an elaborate example of the Spanish Baroque style popular in that era. Vanderbilt's collection of over 17,000 different items of marine interest are displayed. Materials and antiques from Europe were used extensively in the construction of the buildings, and of special interest are several columns near the entry way that came from the ruins of ancient Carthage. Mrs. Vanderbilt's bathroom has a marble tub and solid gold fixtures.

HECKSCHER MUSEUM

Situated in Heckscher Park in Huntington, this bulding was designed by Maynicke & Franks in 1920 to house the art collection of August Heckscher. The building, made of limestone, is of the formal Renaissance Revival style, adhering to accepted academic proportions. The town of Huntington operates the museum which was a gift from the philanthropist. Three large exhibition rooms are filled with representative works of American and European painters. Included in the American section are works by Frederick Edwin Church, George Inness, and Ralph Blakelock and the second largest collection of Thomas Moran in the country. The museum is also used to showcase the work of contemporary Long Island artists.

SUFFOLK COMMUNITY COLLEGE

This "Southampton" building on the college's Selden campus won the silver award in 1973 for architects Bodiecki and Beattie. The college, which offers a two-year program for county residents working towards degrees, also has a group of buildings known as the Plaza of the Towns, each building named after communities of the county.

Land and Seascapes

CHICHESTER ROAD

A youngster enjoys a stroll up this quaint and historic country road in
Huntington. This tree-shaded path conveys a timelessness so prevalent
in the island's landscape. Chichester Road was once a major stagecoach
route from New York City.

AFTER THE STORM

Remnants of a nor'easter in Cold Spring
Harbor.

BARNACLES AT ASHAROKEN

The skeletons of sharks, the long white spines
Of narwhal and of dolphin, bones of men
Shipwrecked, and mighty ribs of foundered barks.
     . . . . from William Cullen Bryant's "Sella"

EBB TIDE

As I ebb'd with the ocean of life,
As I wended the shores I know,
As I walk'd where the ripples continually wash you
   Paumanok,
Where they rustle up hoarse and sibilant,
Where the fierce old mother endlessly cries for her
   castaways,
I musing late in the autumn day, gazing off southward,
Held by this electric self out of the pride of which
   I utter poems,
Was seized by the spirit that trails in the lines
   underfoot,
The rim, the sediment that stands for all the water
   and all the land of the globe!
. . . . Walt Whitman . . . .

NATIVE PINE

A species of pitch pine, this pine native to Long Island springs up
everywhere. In the eastern section of Suffolk County there are
thousands of acres of these trees forming the Pine Barrens, land
which because of its high sand content, is not suitable for producing
anything else. Periodic fires and the bulldozers or the suburban dev-
elopers have cleared out many of these lovely trees, but no harm
can come to those enclosed in the Middle Island Pine Forest Preserve.

CENTERPORT HARBOR WEST

But ever heaves and moans the restless Deep;
    His rising tides I hear,
Afar I see the glimmering billows leap;
    I see them breaking near.
. . . . from William Cullen Bryant's "The Tides"

ROTTED PILING

The beach is cut by the razory ice-wind,
    the wreckguns sound,
The tempest lulls, the moon comes floun-
    dering through the drifts.
. . . . from Walt Whitman's "The Sleepers"

SHORE PINES

Dost thou, oh path of the wood-
  land
End where those waters roar,
Like human life, on a trackless
  beach,
With a boundless Sea before?
. . . .from William Cullen Bryant's
    "The Unknown Way"

HUNTINGTON HARBOR DOCK

The boatmen and clam-diggers
  arose early and stopt for me,
I tuck'd my trouser-ends in my
  boots and went and had a
  good time;
You should have been with us
  that day round the chowder-
  kettle.
. . . .from Walt Whitman's "Song
    of Myself"

HORSES

Long Island has long had a reputation as horse country, and in Colonial times, racing on the Hempstead Plains was a big spectator event. There was competition between Long Island horse breeders and those in Kentucky. Each year a much heralded "North-South" contest drew horse fanciers from all over the island. Some champion horses bred on Long Island include Lady Suffolk, Flora Temple and Messenger.

ARTIST LAKE

Using this beautiful lake in Middle Island as a rendezvous, the Unkechaug and Setalcott Indians named it Blooming Lake for the many water lilies that grew along its shores. Today it is the focal point of a contemporary condominium development. Lake Ronkonkoma, further west, fascinated the Indians who believed it had no bottom. Legend tells of a young Indian Brave, who, distraught over an unrequited love, jumped into Lake Ronkonkoma and committed suicide. Long afterward, legend says, his body was found in a lake in Connecticut!

Commerce and Industry

ST. JAMES RAILROAD STATION

This "gingerbread house" at the Long Island Railroad's
St. James station, on the Port Jefferson line, was built
in 1873 and recently restored to its original condition.
Builder C.L. L'Hommedieu embellished this stationhouse
with convoluted brackets, and a wide roof overhang.

DUTCH ARCHITECTURE

A vestige of the island's early settlers is this former office
of the Northport Trust Company on Northport's Main
Street. It is now a real estate and insurance office. The
stepped gable and the escutcheon suggest Dutch Renaissance, while the first story arch, piers, and second floor
window arches and corbels are Romanesque.

MEADOWBROOK HOSPITAL

This 19 story East Meadow structure, the dynamic care building of the Nassau County Medical Center, is the highest building on Long Island. It cost over $50 million dollars and took three-and-a-half years to build. Max Urbahn and Associates are the architects.

GREAT NECK SHOPPING TOWER

This sleek and distinguished building at 3 Grace Ave., Great Neck, won a 1973 award from the Long Island Association of Commerce and Industry. The architects are Michael Harris Spector and Associates of Great Neck.

CROSSWAYS OFFICE BUILDING

Michael Harris Spector and Associates of Great Neck, are the architects for this prize winning office building in Woodbury. The structure is part of a commercial complex at 7600 Jericho Turnpike known as the Nassau Crossways International Plaza.

LILY-TULIP BUILDING

The Lily-Tulip Division of Owens-Illinois Corporation utilizes this expansive structure on Commack Road in Commack for its research, development, engineering and technical center. The company manufactures paper products.

STONY BROOK POST OFFICE

The post office on Christian Avenue in Stony Brook is the focus of this rustic village. In 1940, residents, deciding that the scattered, and unplanned commercial section of their village was not attractive, rebuilt the entire village in early nineteenth century Federal style. Two semi-circle clusters of shops and offices rest on a gently sloping hill. The post office serves as the center of one cluster, with attached shops stringing out to the right and left. Flower pots hang from the lampposts and flower boxes line the windows of all the shops. The sidewalk is enclosed with a low white railing and the entire village is reminiscent of an earlier time. The building was designed by George Washington Smythe.

SUFFOLK COUNTY OFFICE BUILDING

Though Riverhead is the county seat, its far eastern location makes its use inappropriate, and Hauppauge and Yaphank have become the civic and commercial centers in the county. This office building, designed by Dobiecki, Beatty and Colyer, is in Hauppauge.

FISHING

Another of Long Island's important industries is that of commercial fishing. Over 120 million pounds of fish annually are caught by the commercial enterprises. Not included in this figure are the shellfish for which Long Island is justly famous. In addition, the Long Island bays are filled with amateur fisherman, searching for flounder, porgy and bluefish, making Long Island one of the world's great fishing centers.

HUNTINGTON MANOR FIRE DEPARTMENT

W. Thomas Schaardt is the architect for this
magnificent Egyptian Temple style edifice. It is
one of the largest fire houses on Long Island. It is
located on New York Avenue in Huntington
Station.

FRANKLIN NATIONAL BANK

One of fifty branches, this office of the Franklin National Bank on
Vanderbilt Motor Parkway in Hauppauge, is one of a pair of iden-
tical commercial buildings.

GARDEN CITY HOTEL

Built in 1874 as a country place by the founder of
Garden City, Alexander T. Stewart, this opulent
palace became a hotel two years after his death. The
famous hotel was torn down in the seventies despite
a heroic effort to save it. It has been replaced by a
nine-story apartment building. In its heyday, the
hotel was the meeting place of the famous and infamous. Twenty years after its opening as a hotel,
it was remodeled by Stanford White to include 200
rooms. The remodeling barely finished, it burned to
the ground in 1899. It was promptly rebuilt and
its star-studded clientele returned.

CHRISTMAS TIME IN HUNTINGTON

Loud speakers fill the air with holiday sounds as
last minute shoppers make their way through the
sparkling illumination strung across town.

NEW YORK TELEPHONE COMPANY

The communications center of the New York Telephone Company, on Jericho Turnpike in Huntington, was designed by Rose, Beaton Crosby and Crowe. Its simple proportions stand out on a prominent hilltop.

HEMPSTEAD BANK HEADQUARTERS

A husband and wife team, Frederick and Maria Bentel designed this striking building on Stewart Avenue in Garden City. One of twenty branches on the island, the bank's interior is even more striking than the outside. Curved brick planters and street globe lamps line the lobby interior. Multi-level balconies protrude into the three-story lobby with a wide staircase leading into the first floor offices.

HERITAGE FEDERAL SAVINGS & LOAN ASSOCIATION

This Greenlawn branch of Heritage Savings and Loan shows a successful adaptation of the Colonial style. Architect Harold Greene has demonstrated that a careful combination of landscaping with good design can result in excellence. With headquarters in Huntington, Heritage Federal Savings and Loan was formerly known as Huntington Federal Savings and Loan.

LONG ISLAND DUCKLING

Suffolk County provides two thirds of all the ducks consumed in the United States. On a drive through the eastern end of the island it is impossible not to notice the vast fields of snowy white ducks busily fattening themselves for market. The industry was begun in 1878 and raising ducks is now a major source of revenue.

MID ISLAND SHOPPING PLAZA

One of the first of the sprawling shopping centers on Long Island, this one conveniently located in Hicksville in central Nassau County, offers residents their choice of 95 major department stores and small retail shops, with parking facilities for 6,000 cars.

ROOSEVELT FIELD

This vast shopping center for over 120 stores with parking facilities for 10,000 cars was built on a former air field in Garden City, adjacent to the Meadowbrook Parkway. Originally an open mall, the stores were recently enclosed under air conditioned glass promenades for comfort of shoppers.

SECURITY NATIONAL BANK

The East Hampton branch of this bank was designed by
Robert Dwight Nostrand. Most of Security National
Bank's ninety branches throughout the island adhere to
this Colonial-Georgian style of architecture.

RIVERHEAD SAVINGS BANK

This bank, in the heart of potato farming country was
built in 1923. Its strong limestone columns give it a look
of strength to reassure depositors of the bank's substance.
The Italian Renaissance style building was designed by
architects Holmes, Winslow and Viemeister. At one time,
per capita deposits from potato farmers were the largest
of any in the state, but reduction in agricultural acreage
in the country has had its effect on that.

DIX HILLS FIREHOUSE

This building on Deer Park Rd. was designed by
Harold Greene to house fire apparatus used by
the village firefighters. Firefighting is still done by
volunteers on Long Island, and when the alarm
sounds at the firehouse, volunteers drop what they
are doing and speed to the firehouse to board the
waiting trucks. Though volunteers do not have sirens
on their cars, blue dome lights alert motorists to
clear the roadway.

BANK OF SMITHTOWN

This bank building on Jericho Turnpike in Commack is a prize winner architecturally for designers Ralph Colyer and Edward Everett Post. The innovative design provides a new solution to the problem of drive-in banking. Designers permitted access under the building, thereby eliminating the usual outside window and driveway.

GRUMMAN DATA SYSTEMS CORPORATION

This is the newest of the Grumman buildings, used to house the corporation's complex computer systems. Over one thousand people work in this building with banks of computers, to process not only Grumman's data but that of other firms as well. Employing 25,000 residents of Long Island, the aerospace company, with branches in other areas of the island, is the largest single employer here. The cost of this building in Bethpage was over a million dollars.

NASSAU COLISEUM

This sports arena in Uniondale, somewhat reminiscent of the Coliseum in Rome, was the recipient of an award as the most outstanding building on the island. At a construction cost of over $28 million, the stadium has a seating capacity of 16,000 and occupies the site of the former Mitchel Air Force Base. Designed by Welton Becket and Associates, the Nassau Veterans Memorial Coliseum is used for hockey and basketball games, rock shows and other mass audience events.

LONG ISLAND SAND

Sand and gravel from Long Island is used in the construction of Manhattan skyscrapers, among other things, making the dredging of sand one of the island's most important industries. Barges and trucks carry sand and gravel into New York where it is dispersed to other areas.

HUNTINGTON QUADRANGLE

This modern industrial complex in Melville is one of the largest such facilities built on Long Island to lure business to the area. The architectural theory, in keeping with the low profile suburban area, is to provide sufficient space horizontally as a skyscraper provides vertically.

JOHN F. KENNEDY INTERNATIONAL AIRPORT

This huge airport, ranking second in the world for total number of international passengers served, was originally known as Idlewild International Airport. The name was changed after the death of President John F. Kennedy. Located in southern Queens near the Nassau County border, one of its outstanding features is the TWA terminal, designed by Finnish-American architect Eero Saarinen, who died in 1961.

RELIANCE FEDERAL SAVINGS & LOAN ASSOCIATION

This bank-in-the-round was built in 1967 at I. U. Willets
Road and Willis Avenue in Albertson. Designed by
Siegmund Spiegel, the building demonstrates a pleasing
contemporary design without the fortress effect of so
many financial buildings.

Index

Adelphi University, 108
Albertson, 147
Amityville Public Library, 107
Aquebogue, 10
Artist Lake, 126
Asharoken, 121

Babylon, 38
Baiting Hollow, 91
Bartow House, 13
Bay Shore, 24
Bedlam Street, 35
Bellport Methodist Church, 47
Belmont Park, 92, 93
Benjamin House, 34
Bethpage, 142, 143
Bethpage State Park clubhouse, 81
Brecknock Hall, 68
Bridgehampton, 29
Brookhaven, 47
Brookhaven National Laboratory, 110, 111
Bryant, William Jennings, 69
Bryce Residence, 70
Buell, Rev. Samuel, 28
Buffet House, 7
Buffet House, Old, 9

Calverton, 90
Campanile, The, Robert Moses State Park, 62
Carll Homestead, 4
Carll-Marion Farm, 5
Case-King House, 16
Castro House, 73
Cathedral of the Incarnation, 56, 57
Cedarmere, 69
Centerport, 36, 117
Centerport Harbor, 84, 123
Charter Oaks Country Club, 80
Chichester, James, 40
Chichester Road, 120
Christian Science Church, Huntington, 54
Clinton Academy, 28
Coe Estate, 72
Coe, William R., 72
Cold Spring Harbor, 34, 35, 36, 55, 113
Coliseum, Nassau, 114
Colyer House, 6
Commack, 130, 142, 143
Conklin House, 33
Cooper House, 101
Corwin House, 10
Crossways Office Building, 130
Cupola House, 29
Customs House, Sag Harbor, 22
Cutchogue, 23, 26

Dix Hills Firehouse, 141
Dowling College, 115
Duckling, Long Island, 138

East Hampton, 2, 3, 28, 140
East Nassau Temple, 44
Eaton's Neck Light, 60
Echo Park Pool Complex, 86
Eisenhower Park Clubhouse, 81
Eisenhower Park Memorial, 63
Elm Cottage, 12
Elmhurst, 58
Erasmus Hall High School, 109
Execution Rock Lighthouse, 62

Farmingdale, 94
Fire Island Light, 64
Fishing, 132
Five Gates, 10
Fleet-Goldsmith-Kendrick House, 27
Fleet-Jarvis House, 31
Fowler, Orson Squire, 18
Franklin National Bank, 133
Friends Meeting House, 51

Garden City, 56, 57, 108, 134, 139
Garden City Hotel, 134
Gardiner, Lion, 70
Gardiner, Robert David Lion, 70
Gardiner's Island, 70
Goldsmith-Fleet-Kendrick House, 26
Great Neck Shopping Tower, 128
Gregory House, 14, 15
Greenlawn, 13, 33, 138
Greenport, 39, 68
Grumman Data Systems, 142, 143
Gwathmey House, 67, 68

Halsey House, 35
Hampton House, 29
Hanson House, 67
Hauppauge, 132, 133
Heckscher, August, 82, 118
Heckscher Museum, 118
Heckscher Park, 82
Hempstead, 43, 50, 57, 86
Hempstead Bank Headquarters, 136, 137
Heritage Federal Savings and Loan Association, 138
Hewlett, Lewis House, 7
Hewlett, Thomas, 25
Hicksville, 139
Home Sweet Home, 2, 3
Horses, 92, 93, 125
House By The Sea, 68
Huntington, 4, 6, 7, 8, 9, 10, 11, 12, 14, 15, 17, 19, 26, 31, 33, 42, 51, 54, 67, 82, 118, 120, 124, 134, 135
Huntington Historical Society, 33
Huntington Manor Firehouse, 133
Huntington Quadrangle, 145
Huntington Station, 133
Huntington Yacht Club, 85

Idle Hour, 115

Jared-Wade House, 27
Jarvis-Fleet House, 31
Jayne House, 25
Jericho, 39
Jones Beach, 61, 76, 77, 78, 79

Kauffman, Jay, 5
Kendrick-Fleet-Goldsmith House, 26
Kennedy, John F., International Airport, 146
King House, 16
Kirby House, 104

LaGrange Inn, 38
Lake Grove, 49
Langhans House, 10
Latham, George, 32
Lawrence, 25
Layton Store and House, 100
Levittown, 96
L'Hommedieu House, 6
Lily-Tulip Building, 130

INDEX

Lloyd Harbor, 73
Lloyd Manor, 21
Lloyd's Neck, 21
Locust Valley, 74

Manetto Hill Methodist Church, 50, 98, 99
Manhasset, 20
Manse, Old, 14, 15
Matinecock Farm, 74
Mattituck Church, 49
Mattituck Octagon House, 18
Masonic Temple, Smithtown, 83
Meadowbrook Hospital, 129
Melville, 6, 14, 15, 45, 106
Methodist Church of Hempstead, 57
Middle Island, 128
Middle Island Pine Forest Preserve, 122
Mid-Island Shopping Plaza, 139
Milleridge Inn, 39
Miller Place Library, 32
Montauk, 80
Montauk Light, 63
Montauk Point, 88, 89
Moses, Robert, 62, 78
Mt. Sinai Congregational Church, 48
Muttontown, 80

Nassau Coliseum, 144
Navy-Grumman Airport, 90
Newtown Reformed Church, 58
New Village Congregational Church, 49
New York Telephone Company, 135
Noon Inn, 102
Northport, 128
Northville Grange Hall, 12

Oakdale, 115
Octagon House, Huntington, 20
Octagon House, Mattituck, 18
Old Bethpage, map of, 98
Old Brookville, 116
Old First Church, 42
Old House at Cutchogue, 23
Old Manse, 14, 15
Old South Haven Presbyterian Church, 47
Old Westbury, 32, 51, 71
Old Westbury Gardens, 71
Onderdonk, Henry, 17, 38
Onderdonk House, 20
Orient, 22, 29
Orient Point Light, 60, 61
Oyster Bay, 15, 72

Parrish Art Museum, 112
Payne, John Howard, 2, 3
Peace and Plenty Inn, 40
Phipps, John S., 71
Port Washington, 96
Post College Library, 116
Post, C. W., 116
Potter, Gilbert, House, 4
Potter, John S., House, 71
Powell Farm, 102
Powell House, 17
Presbyterian Church of Setauket, 44
Prime, Cornelia, 9
Prime Octagon House, 20

Quakers, 51

Raynham Hall, 15
Reliance Federal Savings and Loan Association, 147
Republic Aviation, 94
Rich House, 11
Riverhead, 34, 140
Riverhead Savings Bank, 140
Rock Hall, 25
Rocky Point, 53
Rogers, Nathan, 29
Roosevelt Field, 139
Roosevelt Raceway, 95
Roslyn, 5, 17, 21, 38, 69, 70
Roslyn Grist Mill, 17
Roslyn Village Hall, 5

Sag Harbor, 22, 27, 48
Sag Harbor Customs House, 22
Sagtikos Manor, 24
St. George Episcopal Church, 43
St. George, Manor of, 30
St. George Parish House, 50
St. James Episcopal Church, 52
St. James Railroad Station, 128
St. John's Episcopal Church, 55
Sammis House, 26
Sands House, 15
Sands Point, 15
Security National Bank, 140
Selden, 118
Setauket, 25, 26, 44
Setauket Presbyterian Church, 44
Shelter Island, 30
Sherwood-Jayne House, 25
Smith, Joel Barnum, House, 33
Smith, Solomon, House, 8
Smith, William 'Tangier', 30
Smithtown, Bank of, 142, 143
Smithtown High School, 112
Smithtown Masonic Temple, 83
Smithtown Presbyterian Church, 45
Society for the Preservation of Long Island Antiquities, 26
Southampton, 36, 69, 112
South Haven, Old Presbyterian Church, 47
Southold, 16, 46
Southold Universalist Church, 46
State University at Stony Brook, 114
Stewart, Alexander T., 56, 57, 134
Stony Brook Post Office, 131
Suffolk Community College, 118
Suffolk County Office Building, 132
Sunquam Elementary School, 106
Suydham House, 36
Sweet Hollow Presbyterian Church, 45
Sylvester Manor, 30
Syosset, 44

Thompson, Benjamin, 26
Thompson House, 26
Townsend Manor, 39
Trinity Evangelical Lutheran Church, 53

Uniondale, 144
Universalist Church, 51

Valentine House, 5
Valentine-Obadiah Washington House, 21
Van Cortlandt, Stephanus, 24
Vanderbilt Museum, 117
Vanderbilt, William K., 115

INDEX

Vanderbilt, William K. II, 117
Villas, The, 80

Wade House, Jared, 27
Washington Manor, 38
Washington, Obadiah-Valentine House, 21
Webb House, 22
West Hills, 40

Whalers' Presbyterian Church, 48
Whaling Museum, 113
White, Stanford, 69, 134
Whitman, Walt, Birthplace, 19
Williams House and Carpenter Shop, 103
Willow Mere, 5
Witkin House, 66
Woodbury, 130

CREDITS